EACH STEP A DISCOVERY

(A Collection of Miniatures)

by Michael L. Newell

Acknowledgements

Many of these poems (sometimes in a different form) have previously appeared in the following periodicals, to whose editors grateful acknowledgement is made: *The Aurorean*; *Bakunin*; *Basho's Road*; *Bear Creek Haiku*; *Bellowing Ark*; *Current*; *The Haiku Foundation: Per Diem Archives*; *Issa's Untidy Hut*; *Lilliput Review*; *Muse of Fire*; *Potpourri*; *Shemom*; *Three Line Poetry*; *Verse-Virtual*; *Wild Plum--A Haiku Journal*.

I would like to thank the following fellow poets for their support and generosity over the years: Dan Franch; Michael Minassian; Ed Ruzicka; and Robert Wexelblatt.

A special thanks is extended to Anna and Michael Citrino for decades of support.

Certain small press editor/publishers deserve a tip of the hat for all they have done for me and other small press poets: the late Firestone Feinberg; Peggy French; Jack Hart; Joe Maita; Phil Wagner; the late Robert R. Ward; and Don Wentworth.

Cover artwork: Anna Citrino.
Author Photo: Michael Citrino

AUTHOR'S FOREWORD

This is a book of what I call miniatures. They are short form poetry. They are anywhere from two to twenty lines long, although the longer pieces generally consist of several shorter sections. Most of these poems are only a few lines long.

The vast majority of poems I write are longer than those found in this book. These poems began, about thirty years ago, as an attempt to achieve as much compression as I could in a poem.

Some of these have appeared in haiku magazines, but I have never considered any of my work to be haiku, neither Japanese nor American haiku. I was simply striving for compression.

Over time I developed a love for East Asian poetry: Basho, Buson, Issa, Tu Fu (Du Fu), Li Po (Li Bo), and Wang Wei. These poets influenced my work inevitably, but no more so than short form work done by American short form poets such as poet/editor Don Wentworth, Tom Montag, the later work of Robert Sund, and the translations by Kenneth Rexroth of Chinese and Japanese poetry. I suppose one might say that many of my miniatures are second or third cousins to haiku, but also reflect my own wide travels and life experiences in thirteen different countries and thirteen different American states.

--Michael L. Newell

This book is dedicated to my closest friend since my days in college: Joseph Glaser, a fine musician, a first-rate thinker, and a gentle soul who is filled with great compassion for all around him.

TEN MINIATURES ON A THEME

I.
my pen leaks words
which intrigue a stranger
unexpected delight

II.
my pen leaks words
describing things unseen
by me

III.
my pen leaks words
which amaze and delight
when meant to cause fright

IV.
my pen leaks words
that cause tears of joy
yet annoy the pen

V.
I depend on my pen
to excavate things beyond
my understanding

VI.
My pen is independent
of my will. It goes
where it pleases.

VII.
My pen is often cranky,
refuses my suggestions,
demands to take a nap.

VIII.
My pen frequently decides
the path we will
take together.

IX.
At times I will in anger
store my pen in a drawer.
This seldom lasts long.

X.
Without my pen, I
am speechless. It knows
how to form needed words.

roses at midnight
her startled face
a shower of stars

silent inside a quiet rain
a tree, a woman,
and me

A WINTER'S SONG

few leaves left
streets bereft of friends
rain wind and I alone
alone alone-o

in slow rain where creeks thread farms
my breath flows with ease
of crisp dawn breeze

I dampen in slow rain.
Breath flows with rhythm of waters.
I could hear a snail crawl.

stained glass panes
butterfly wings
fallen on crabgrass

on park bench old man
draped by gloaming leans into
oncoming darkness

Old man slumped on park bench
wears tattered coat,
fades slowly into dusk.

birdsong and golden light
wash my bedroom
I bathe in hope for the day

crepuscule deepens
crow on window sill fades
tomorrow's a stranger

rough hewn hands lifted aloft
by brawny arms
mountains cradle La Paz

every tear has a story
some brief
some last a lifetime

mist curtains afternoon
faces bloom and vanish
life stories pass

in large party with friends
silence is deafening

midnight silence
stars fill sky in cold witness
again I face myself

one brown curled leaf
in violent rainstorm
my future waiting

in gloaming a wee lass
runs uphill singing
toward her future

girl leads leaping goat on rope
down muddy spring street
onlookers roar

lightly it lit on her thumb
the smiling child
two free creatures

wind embraces neighborhood
trees and bushes swing and sway
dance fever

wild geese in flocking
conversation   an old couple
glance up and laugh

lost again in thickets
of language what is this
obsession with words

another day another mistake
another path to wander

beyond distant fields
cars swim through twilight
lives floating past

two streets over, moon
snared in tree branches
in concert with snarling cat

daylight fades
I no longer recognize
face in mirror

fireflies flicker in dark
everywhere one looks
haiku haiku haiku

perched on rickety fence
battered old tomcat
and midnight moon

small girl cartwheels
down hallway out the door
summer   at long last

all day wind rain empty streets
where I wander lost
in weather's wonder

shafts of moonlight
sewn by slanting needles
icy autumn rain

child's face in window
bathed by golden moonlight
life awaits

crooked smile in mirror
my father's ghost

day breaks in deep scarlet wave;
poised in meadow: listen--
far cry of deer

Each song sung
by bird or man
charts a universe.

WINTER'S EMBRACE

he naps on dawn porch
white hair matches snow
enveloping lawns and streets

rambling empty dawn streets
wrapped in icy autumn air
abrupt downpour

DRUMBEATS

fade
into
distance:

your heart,
my heart,
heart of the world.

her hand brushes his cheek
flower starts to grow within

startled by lightning flash
he falls in love anew
with her sudden smile

whisper of warmth
in rainy breeze
spring is at the door

through open window
moonlight finds a home
in half-filled teacup

birdsong at dusk fills
drenched streets, echoes
in my mind for hours

in absolute stillness, bird
and man stare at one another;
time stops.

shafts of moonlight sift
through swift-flying clouds
illuminate a child's face

AWE

in the cathedral hush of starlight
fingers brush and unite
shelter in the presence of the infinite

beneath stars
mountains loom
always another hill to climb

BEAUTY'S EMBRACE

a Monarch Butterfly enthroned
on a fingertip

AUTUMN SONG

swaying from a wintry branch,
one final golden leaf--
all beauty contains grief.

And The Rain It Rains All Through The Day

Down the plains of my window,
wet sleds ferry their freight,
years of grief.

bending with wind
old man hums work song
struggles uphill

battered tweed cap
cocked jauntily
we ramble through all weather

As she leaves,
rain stitches my grief
onto huge sleeve of uncaring night.

It was the face within the face
that caught my eye,
the boy within the man.

always mockery
thirteen countries
thirteen encounters with crow

DISCOVERY

smooth and cool
        as a slow moving

stream in spring
        flowing across bare legs

your skin
        in morning sunlight

A SUITE OF RAIN MINIATURES

I.

rainy season has arrived
sleep comes more easily

II.

fusillade of rain
heads down
even children seek shelter

III.

walking down muddy road
in steady rain
feet beating time to drops

IV.

body aching
I fall asleep
wake to rain's tattoo on window

V.

tonight I grieve the loss
of an old friend
rain softly joins me

VI.

children splash soccer ball
up and down rainy street
leaning on wall, we chuckle

VII.

cranky rooster in rain
chases other birds away
won't move for me

VIII.

my old friend the rain
joins wind
in frenzied dance

IX.

morning mist anoints the day
in silent damp
I pray all will be blessed

X.

rain thunder and wind
again my friends come calling
I join them apace

Kigali, Rwanda, October 2011

SONGS OF A NOMAD

Hail shakes the window;
soon I'll don boots and slicker
to trudge through wet snow.

*

Stirring coals, her youth
envelops the room, such warmth;
the wind coughs through eaves.

*

Guitar unstrung hums
in a dust-filled corner, voice
rusty from disuse.

*

Hot meal, savory:
chicken, rice, giblet gravy;
soon, stale bread--cold cans.

*

Family dances:
fiddle, banjo, strong voices;
last glance from the door.

*

Woolen cap pulled low;
tossing twigs onto a blaze;
moon lights distant farms.

*

Iced branches crackle;
dark wind sprays fine white powder;
chimes infuse the night.

ALWAYS THE MOON: A SUITE OF MINIATURES

1.

wind
rain drops
a floating moon

2.

clouds
wind blown
veil the moon

3.

a vanishing moon
above mountains
sun

4.

howling
bereft hound
alone with moon

5.

strangers
you me
a blue moon

6.

the moon hovers
over valley
silence

7.

in midnight lightning
the moon
appears

Above La Paz a hawk
glides upon same wind
with which I wrestle.

Windblown rain-rusted
merry-go-round drifts in fog,
creaks across decades.

final embers of day
hint at what was
and what is to come

Old man slowly rocks;
clock of his face
ticks toward midnight.

Most eloquent
when simplest
the grammar of touch.

distant hills through rain
all my yesterdays
fading to night

children's voices filtered
through steady rain
the past always with me

dusk's embers linger
old man on park bench
barely visible

old man in mirror
who are you
how did we get here

wind flutes through eaves
all afternoon a widow
whispers one name one name

With hope,
a fisherman casts his lure
in search of possibility.

Bereft of forest,
wind, and rain, a fiddle sings
a song of exile.

in bare field three trees
slow dance in wind
as last leaves of autumn depart

moonlight floats in glass
of red wine all night I dream
of my lover's smile

all through winter afternoon
scent of autumn
leaf smoke from neighbor's yard

Another decade gone.
Head and chin grizzled,
I welcome icy rain.

autumn wind whistles
across train tracks, lifts fallen
leaves -- wistful ballet

lost in wind-blown trees
solitary thought
astray in forest's song

my pen leaks words
which intrigue a stranger
unexpected delight

roaming densely forested ridge
eyes discover
a home in shadows

as I rock on my balcony
a full moon spills
across my lap

shafts of moonlight
sewn by slanting needles
icy autumn rain

silent
in a meadow
everywhere a symphony

slow dancing late night cafe
sudden applause
a drunk in the window

slow falling snow fills
my footprints, blots out
my past

splashed by light and sound
golden moon and wild Irish fiddle
dance feet dance

stray cat hisses, bats
at shaft of moonlight
my sentiments exactly

walking slowly to nowhere
each step
a discovery

wild array of colors
fills yard
parliament of flowers

wind and rain lashed
solitary walker
it was midnight at noon

wind sings through broken guitar strings
I see a rose a fireplace
your smile

collisions on icy autumn fields
crunch of bone and muscle
proof of life

fat stranger in window slouches;
hair thinned, beard grizzled,
damn   it's me.

whist whist whist whispered
wind at my window
and I ceased my complaints

a child at dawn
two births
only one will be repeated

A flowering rock.
Why do I insist
on questioning miracle?

FOR LILY

a girl hums, pens an essay
she'd cheerfully burn,
chews two sticks of gum

A road loops, twists, falls
down a long hill,
its end ever receding.

Above heating pipes
buried in deep snow drifts,
rabbits huddle.

across silent decades
wind in photo swirls leaves
and ruffles your hair

all man's grief in a drop of rain
his hope a glistening leaf

all night the cruel city
lay naked
beneath cleansing rain

all night the moon
sleeps in a boxcar
trailing a river of light

ally ally in come free
down the street
my past calls

alone in night
fog with nothing to curl around
or brush against

an old couple strolls the street
arms and hips brushing
a hymn of love

Man on bass has left the room.
His fingers still
dance along strings.

Beneath a setting sun
three trees danced--
do you remember?

birth:
a falling
toward silence

blown butterfly
with stained glass wings
sails into   out of my life

cities at night,
drugged animals
awaiting scalpel or saw

Crack of thunder wakes me
on my porch, life
demanding attention.

Crow, old friend,
whom do you scold today--
me again, or any who pass?

dark whiskey memory
and desire
where did the night go

dawn to dusk
rain stitches a seamless day
stand with me beneath the oak

distant dust plume
long dirt road and old Studebaker
fade from sight

each hour seeds the next
and so on and so forth
and thus tomorrow

each moment contains
ashes of the past
and seeds of the future

Each step,
slow or swift, lasts
a lifetime.

each word is a prayer
for forgiveness
silence always the answer

evening rain infiltrates trees
in back yard
where two sip whiskey and the past

evening sunlight splashes
across child's rapt face
dancing to her own song

every tear has a story
some brief
some last a lifetime

father's hands, gnarled leathery clumps,
how to put them on,
become a man

frog in shoe
won't budge
why am I laughing

from life's daily prose
I filch minutes
to invest in hope's poetry

Heinz Holliger's oboe
playing Bach
moonlight on fresh fallen snow

how often words accuse others
yet describe self
pied crow complaining

I erase one more bad poem
soon I too
will vanish from memory

Lengthening through wide yard,
watered by nearby sprinkler,
a child's shadow.

midnight silence
stars fill sky in cold witness
again I face myself

nibbled slowly
a daily poem for breakfast
such luxury

One of life's mysteries:
her damp thigh shimmers
beneath rain drenched tree.

Outside my window schoolgirls
chant rhymes and dance.
So many vanished years.

in rainy evening gloom
two lads slide through puddles
some things never change

Sad-eyed, exhausted,
stoop-shouldered wife (child in arms),
kinder than spring rain.

She touched his shoulder.
Dawn broke across his face.
Love's quiet moments.

Speaking or walking,
everything you do
has a lilt, a bounce, my friend.

splintered porch where wind
rocks abandoned chair
so many years gone by

across midnight pasture
stars bloom
eyes hungrily graze

sun fills one side of a valley
rain the other
I'm lost in the sky

voluptuous nymph,
the moon, artfully draped
in a thin dark tunic

Wind winds wintry fingers round
my heart. I think of you
and all is spring.

all day wind rain empty streets
where I wander lost
in weather's wonder

golden midnight moon
rides ocean waves
its light trumpets unfettered love

all week mother and father visit
my dreams nothing is said
they just shake their heads
faces full of disapproval

fiddle aches for
abandoned forest
mourns with exile's song

enveloped by rain
I swirl and sing
alone in a drowning world

lad on father's shoulders
floats through wheat field
hair adrift in evening wind

deep in humming creek, golden moon
bestows grace throughout
midnight neighborhood

moonlight floats through upstairs window
tumbles down stairs
out cracked front door

huge rocks flower high overhead
where condors soar
awe spreads its cloak

full moon ripples
in green tea stirred by wind
old man on porch slowly rocks

Wind loves tree and bush;
birds love tree limbs, rooftops;
I love your quiet smile.

lizard swaggers across lawn
when we meet
he stares me down

family wonders
what's wrong with me
question I often ask myself

crescent moon sails across
tree-lined hills as loons
sing from windblown creek reeds

pebble in shoe
too lazy to remove
easier to buy new shoe

dark clouds fill horizon
lightning scrawls warning
new year arrives

snared in tree branches
golden half-moon snarling cat
and abandoned kite

lost in rain's steady murmur
complaints swallowed
crow and I sit speechless

spicy   dramatic
his radishes
his choice in women

grapes held in farmer's hands
succulent firm perfect
his poems his life

Labrador barks at her image
in pond as dusk
swallows afternoon

reflected in a tea cup
half-moon sailing over
forested hills

roof carpenter curses rain
as hammer slips
breaks finger

lad sits in canoe
fishing line still in still water
strums blues guitar

spring breeze cool
comfort under sun
I slumber in grass cradle

face submerged in icy wind
I trudge toward tomorrow
geese sweep past

drenched with summer sweat
grizzled gent leans against oak
inhales river breeze

Pied crow scolds
old man eating on porch
where's my grub, bub

He rises, face to wind,
inhales scent of future,
yet tastes the past.

firefly lands on fingertip
of wee lass at dusk
swift intake of breath

moon is so cold tonight
I wear two coats
in his honor

Beethoven summons dawn
Bach lures dusk
at noon I'm wistful for Liszt

let our quarrel end
as we sip cider in canoe
on village pond

Wet and half-blind
in dawn mist, I
give thanks for morning birdsong.

heron suspended over creek
in dusk mist
in silence I bow

Bach flows from neighbor's home
dances with dawn on lawn
cat chases slippery shadows

surprise visitor in
settling dusk
nomadic butterfly

crows in disputation
wild cacophony
why do I laugh so hard

strange motif
finding myself repeatedly
without recognition

stranger in passing window
makes me laugh
damn   it's my own image

through crack in concrete
solitary flower
sways in breeze

autumn wind soughs
through palm and pine
music majestic and divine

deep in leaves black cat
motionless on branch
contemplates riot of crows

calligraphy of clouds
etched across sky
define oncoming day

middle of muddy road
rooster and I locked in stare down
rain streams past

gecko in grass
vanishes as I pass
I doff my cap   walk on

wearing clerical collar
pied crow scolds
passersby who ignore him

night silence swallows
ancient on porch sipping wine
silently rocking

old woman slowly knitting,
rocking in doorway,
fades into gloaming

a stranger to the land --
fact which names me
in many ways

sudden rain urges
I walk faster
I refuse, lift face skyward

Rush of rain sweeps
street clean of people
alone I sing with abandon

alone on log
still heron
sudden strike   fish dinner

sudden yellow blossom
full moon in trees
I toast the night

lightning flashes
sudden discovery
life continues

glass of red wine
enriched by full moon
ah, drunk on life and world

wild the wind and rain
as I explore new locale
exuberant my laughter

CELEBRATE

wind through window
rain on roof
I clumsily dance
round living room
fill night
with hoarse song

crepuscule deepens
crow on window sill fades
tomorrow's a stranger

all afternoon steady breeze
eases heat
stirs fur of lazy cat

small black bird wind-spun
into erratic flight
beauty's wild dance

Unable to settle,
leaf leaps
gust to gust.

wind's ragged fingers
toss morning into disarray
crow complains

lost and alone
one leaf sailing air
between tree and street

she slips into shower
dolphin returning home
to silken water

my arm her pillow
as we sprawl in summer grass
beneath windblown sun

borne upon ocean waves
wild psalm of infinite praise
as sun rises

leaves admired this morning
coat the ground with shattered gold
autumn flames

trapped in flowering branches
a quarter moon
a lost cat and I

on the porch he slips away
with vanishing years
into haunting dusk

the sun that golden pilgrim
lays hands upon my face
forgives misspent years

A leaf floats across street.
I have floated between continents.
Kinsmen.

When I look at my father's picture,
I hear whispers,
mourn things undone.

beneath breath of midnight rain
above my bed
I am still a child

MIDNIGHT FOOTNOTE TO LOVEMAKING

The snail's path across
our bedroom windowpane wakes
us with its shrieking.

GROTTO

That deep wound, that gorge,
where all lost loves and beliefs
flower in the steady
rain of inconsolable memory;

those who visit and stay
too long disappear
and return only
in the cruel rains of autumn.

in the mirror a stranger
I wander off
in search of self

YES!

You. Again.
Faint perfume,
your hair
against my jaw,

softening a hard
bony ridge. You.
Again. And
Again. Yes!

DEPARTURE

The damp petal lingers, adheres
to fingers;

I flick it
away, some of my flesh

clinging to its flight
into rough grass,

and I turn
to embrace the spring

wind in my face,
the long road ahead.

LA PAZ

the bowl of the mountains' hands
lifts the city skyward--
an ancient offering

HER SMILE

starlight filling an earthen jar
on a moonlit mesa

I listen to old fiddler.
In silence between notes
a heartbeat.

FRONT AND BACK

A double shadow:
Future   Past.

MIDNIGHT SNACK

The sky tonight is dusted with stars,
snow blown across a vast window;
children on rooftops go bundled
picking the biggest stars to throw
like blackberries into old jelly jars.
Every third one they eat in wonder.
Those old cold flames make bellies thunder.

MIDNIGHT RAIN

Water is falling again, a comfort
from the womb, this wet

rocking, rocking, rocking
of rooms and all within.

early morning streets
two alone
a soft rain and I

time means nothing
yet is all I have
to share with you

a flower splits concrete
your smile nudges its way
into my bleak thoughts

each tree I pass is
a woman I once knew
the past ever present

An hour spent
in company of a friend,
time beyond value.

wind stirs coffee, faces
bloom in mist, gulls ghost past,
ceaseless, waves roam beach

golden moon sails
over mountain peak
my heart as cargo

NO!

Yet another way
to say Yes.

Snowstorm

Eyes in window, only
things moving not white
in night.

In full-throated chorus across Tashkent skies,
an armada stains early light--
crows, crows, crows.

conversation ends
a candle extinguished
in the dark again

Moon, old friend of love's tides,
tugs at her blood,
on her lips a hint of wine.

her only thought all day
erotic whispers
of wind teasing leaves

what crazed painter has traced
his heart upon night sky--
such wild brushstrokes

parchment skin of old folk
candlelit from within
life's final embers

A BUTTERFLY

Feel its warmth
        (fragile as a thought
                    blooming)
      light on a shoulder,
hear it (a wisp of
                    memory?)
        settling in
to comfort.

lying in hammock
amidst murmur of bees
breeze redolent of wine

autumn moon floats in silence
above midnight rain
train tracks glisten

MIDNIGHT FANTASY

When a full moon rows a silvery path
across an evening sky, I imagine

hitching a ride (along with Li Po)
above the local creek filled

with otters, fish, waterfowl and moonglow,
and taking a long dive from high above,

wind whistling as we prepare to break
the surface and discover an unknown future.

reflections in windows along streets
life's path in series of snapshots

meandering tumbling a leaf's
journey, wind tossed to earth.
my future.

A lad stutter stepped
down side street, hair aflame,
Scott Joplin in his feet.

a weed cracks concrete
a toddler's chuckle unfreezes
my stony face

firefly poised on child's palm
a hint of joining
never consummated

huge rocks flower high overhead
where condors soar
awe spreads its cloak

storm swirls through pine and palm
trees turn into wind-organs
birds whirl in wild ballet

weight of fallen leaves
thousand regrets unnamed
no flame enough to burn

even wind ceases its song
to listen to moon's
celestial tunes

GOING HOME

truant old man lost
in remnants of gloaming
fades into woodland
next to river

Buffeted by winds of time
and scorn of the young, an old man
cloaks himself in silence.

saddest eyes on train
caged dog whose tail thumps
with rhythm of rails

Stooped and slow,
she shuffles to work
in her kingdom of flowers.

rain chuckles in tree leaves
above a couple slowly kissing

butterflies flutter by
why do I so seldom
notice

Breeze, puddles, rain, grizzled ancient,
quartet adrift
in midnight light.

every day is borrowed
until there are no more
time's tides await me

Autumn fields replete
with shattered leaves of gold.
All all foretells our end.

Touching one another
in night, even at seventy,
they blossom.

Spring arrives, trills song
of flowers unleashing
their colorful ballet.

wildly warbled melody of one
shy invisible bird elicits dance steps
from my clumsy feet navigating
muddy Kigali street on a work day morning
such song is better than wine

MOTH

in lamp light
crazed with unutterable

desire

drawn to immolation
wings sing love love love

FANDANGOS

1.

wirehaired fox terriers
skim the earth
like flat stones skipped over water
feet scarcely brush the surface
who knew dogs could dance

2.

cats
preside over gravity effortlessly
leap six feet to land on fence tops
show no more strain than when
stepping from ground to perch
on a six inch high step
casual navigators of the air
all space is theirs to command

3.

Tom Stoppard
does his routines
on uneven parallel bars
of English language
flips soars twists turns drops
rises somersaults surprises
reinvents what is possible
leaves spectators open-mouthed
begging for more
even his departures to silence
are elegant speech

DUSK IN REEDSPORT

Loons at nightfall dive
deep into creek; I too would
vanish into deep.

Wind's brawny arms wrap
me round, guide me slowly home;
rain blesses my steps.

From behind me, loons
cry through the gloaming; their calls
rise, fall, haunting me.

FOUR VOICES

the first one said life is a breath of air
which we have barely time to savor

another said life is a flower which blooms
in the rain and dies in the dry season

I muttered life is a thought lost in a library
with no book or shelf for shelter

and she said life is my son and daughter
and the time we will share together.

Kigali, Rwanda, January 2012

WALKING SMALL TOWN BACKSTREETS

I encounter waves of honeysuckle scent from nearby
fields ringed round by blackberry bushes; bless memory,
as it now recalls choirs of bairns in the gloaming, as they
called to one another and ran hither and thither,
swarms of fireflies that ignited their imaginations,
and parents on neighborhood porches who watched
all their shenanigans with a tolerant eye as they slowly
rocked, sipped iced tea, and recalled their own youth.

BOY AT WINDOW

stares into long afternoon
rain stitches meadow forest and sidewalk
seamlessly together
all of life awaits

empty fields cracked concrete
abandoned school
faint chants and cries of children

daylight fades
I no longer recognize
face in mirror

Michael L. Newell was born in Florida in 1945. In addition to living in thirteen states, he has lived in Japan, The Philippine Islands, Thailand, The United Arab Emirates, Jordan, Kuwait, Uzbekistan, Mexico, Egypt, Estonia, Saudi Arabia, Bolivia, and Rwanda. He currently lives in a small town on the Florida coast.

Newell studied writing with Benjamin Saltman and Ann Stanford. His poems have appeared in a number of periodicals including *Aethlon: The Journal of Sport Literature*; *Bellowing Ark*; *College English*; *Current*; *English Journal*; *First Class*; *The Iconoclast*; *Issa's Untidy Hut*; *Jerry Jazz Musician*; *Lilliput Review*; *Poetry Depth Quarterly*; *Rattle*; *Shemom*; *Ship of Fools*; *Tulane Review*; and *Verse-Virtual*.

Some of his previous books include *A Stranger to the Land*; *Seeking Shelter*; *A Long Time Traveling*; *Traveling without Compass or Map*; *Meditation of an Old Man Standing on a Bridge*; and *Wandering*.

9 789390 202119